A Photo Tour Of Chicago

Photographs by Christian Heeb, text by Alan J. Shannon and Andrew Hudson, layout by Andrew Hudson. Published by Photo Tour Books, Inc. Printed in 2008. (First published May 2005; reprinted with updates in 2006 and 2008.)

ISBNs: Paperback: 978-1-930495-05-0
                Hardcover: 978-1-930495-06-7

To license these images, please visit heebphoto.com

To order more books, call 858-780-9726 or send an email from phototourbooks.com.

Cameras used: Nikon F5, Asahi Pentax 6x7, Nikon F100, Nikon F90s, Nikon Coolpix 5000, Nikon D1-X.

The pictures consist of: 84 color photos, 2 duotone photos, 9 black-and-white photos, 1 color map.

Additional photos by Brett Shoaf and Charlie Manz of Artistic Visuals. artisticvisuals.com

Cover photo: Chicago skyline from the platform at Milton Lee Olive Park.

The photographer thanks Julia Latka of America Journal for her help and encouragment. The publisher thanks Chai Lee of The Art Institute of Chicago; Bobbi McLaughlin for proof reading; and Greg Lee and Mark Lopez of Imago.

"The Magnificent Mile" is a trademark of the Greater North Michigan Avenue Association.

Published by:
Photo Tour Books, Inc.
9582 Vista Tercera
San Diego CA 92129
Tel: 858-780-9726
phototourbooks.com

Distributed to the trade by:
National Book Network
(NBN), tel: 800-462-6420.
Lanham MD 20706
nbnbooks.com

Production by Imago (U.S.). Prepress by Bright Arts (H.K.). Printed in China.

A Photo Tour of
CHICAGO

Photographs by
Christian Heeb

Text by Alan J. Shannon

CONTENTS

INTRODUCTION

"Make no little plans;
they have no magic to stir men's blood...
Make big plans, aim high in hope and work."
—Daniel Hudson Burnham,
Chicago city planner (1846–1912).

The **Windy City,** the City of Big Shoulders, the Second City, even Hog Butcher of the World—Chicago has many nicknames. But perhaps the city's Latin motto, *Urbs in Horto*—or City in a Garden—is its most fitting. Collared by 29 miles of lakefront parks and 550 neighborhood parks, this undeniably urbane city of many identities lives up to its motto.

Chicago embraces visually-dominant Lake Michigan, one of the largest bodies of fresh water in the world. From its perch at the mouth of the Chicago River, this quintessentially American city has nestled itself firmly along the lake's beaches and shoreline.

Following Burnham's oft-repeated dictum to "make no little plans," Chicago has pursued a path of innovation and splendor in its efforts to create a city worthy of its celebrated favorite sons such as Louis Sullivan, Frank Lloyd Wright and Mies van der Rohe. The result is a city of stunning, soul-stirring vistas wrought by both man and nature.

Chicago was founded as a fur-trading post; gained prominence as the country's grain, meat-packing and transportation hub; and is now the country's third-largest city.

"It is hopeless for the occasional visitor to try to keep up with Chicago—she outgrows her prophecies faster than she can make them. She is always a novelty; for she is never the Chicago you saw when you passed through the last time."
—Mark Twain, 'Life On The Mississippi,' 1883.

HISTORY

From Marshland to Metropolis

Pre-1673 Potawatomi Indians inhabit the area, calling the river marshlands "Checaugou," meaning "wild onion" or "skunk cabbage," which could be found there.

1673 The name "Chicago" first appears on maps following the visit of French missionary Jacques Marquette and French-Canadian explorer Louis Joliet.

1779 The area's first non-Indian resident is Jean Baptiste Point du Sable, an African-American trader from the Caribbean, who builds a house at the mouth of the Chicago River, near today's Wrigley Building.

1795 Chicago becomes American following a treaty with Indian tribes.

1833 The city of Chicago is incorporated with a population of 350.

1858 With canals and railroads connecting the Mid-West to the Great Lakes and New York, Chicago becomes America's transportation hub.

1869 Chicago's first elevated train—today's "L"—was attempted. Between 1872 and 1900, 70 companies were created to provide elevated rail systems.

1871 The Great Chicago Fire burns most downtown buildings.

1884 The first skyscraper is built. The ten-story Home Insurance Building (1885, demolished 1931) was supported by a "Chicago skeleton" of steel girders rather than thick masonry walls.

1897 Charles Tyson Yerkes completes the Union Elevated Train Loop, today's "Loop" that encircles the downtown area.

1893 The World's Columbian Exposition draws 27 million visitors—almost half of the nation's population. The "Great White City" of Greek- and Roman-inspired buildings heralds a Beaux-Arts "City Beautiful" movement.

1900 The flow of the Chicago River is reversed, to carry sewage away from the lake and down a 28-mile canal to Lockport, IL and the Gulf of Mexico.

1909 Daniel Hudson Burnham's Plan of Chicago proposes river-front public spaces and wide boulevards.

1910–1930 The "Great Migration" from the South to the North increases Chicago's African-American population from 44,000 to 235,000. Delta blues music brings jazz in the 1920s (with Jelly Roll Morton, Louis Armstrong), swing in the 1930s (Benny Goodman), and electric blues in the 1940s (Muddy Waters, Howlin' Wolf, Buddy Guy).

1920–1933 Prohibition and bootlegging is a multi-million dollar business for Chicago's gangsters.

1931	Chased by Eliot Ness and "The Untouchables," gangster Al Capone gets convicted—of tax evasion.
1941	Enrico Fermi at the University of Chicago starts the nuclear age with the first controlled atomic nuclear chain reaction.
1943	Ike Sewell creates the Chicago-style deep-dish pizza at Pizzeria Uno.
1949	TV soap operas begin in Chicago with "These Are My Children" for NBC.
1953	Hugh Hefner prints the first "Playboy" magazine.
1955	Ray Kroc opens the first franchised McDonald's in Des Plaines.
1971	The 110-story Sears Tower opens. It was, and is today, American's tallest building.
1993	Chicagoan Carol Moseley-Braun becomes the first African-American U.S. senator.
2004	Chicago's Millennium Park opens.

NICKNAMES

Windy City. The moniker was first used in 1885 as a travel advertisement, when Chicago was promoted as a summer resort destination due to the cooling breezes off Lake Michigan. The nickname was popularized in 1893 when New York Sun editor Charles Dana, tired of hearing Chicagoans boast of the Columbian Exposition, wrote "Don't pay attention to the nonsensical claims of that windy city."

Second City. Chicago rose to prominence as the nation's second city in population, after New York. However, the term Second City gained fame from a derisive article in the New Yorker in 1952. Since 1990, Los Angeles has relegated Chicago to third city status.

CHICAGO BORN

The city and suburbs of Chicago were the birthplaces of: Edgar Rice Burroughs (1875), Raymond Chandler (1888), Ernest Hemingway (1899), Walt Disney (1901), Eliot Ness (1903), Benny Goodman (1909), Betty Ford (1918), Mel Tormé (1925), Hugh Hefner (1926), Bob Fosse (1927), Philip K. Dick (1928), Quincy Jones (1933), Herbie Hancock (1940), Raquel Welch (1940), Harrison Ford (1942), Peter Cetera (1944), Harold Ramis (1944), Hillary Rodham Clinton (1947), David Mamet (1947), Carol Moseley-Braun (1947), John Belushi (1949), Gary Shandling (1949), Scott Turow (1949), Bill Murray (1950), Mr. T (1950), John Landis (1950), Suze Orman (1951), Robin Williams (1951), Robert Zemeckis (1952), Frances McDormand (1957), Michael Flatley (1958), Bernie Mac (1958), Daryl Hannah (1960), Bonnie Hunt (1964), John Cusack (1966), and Gillian Anderson (1968).

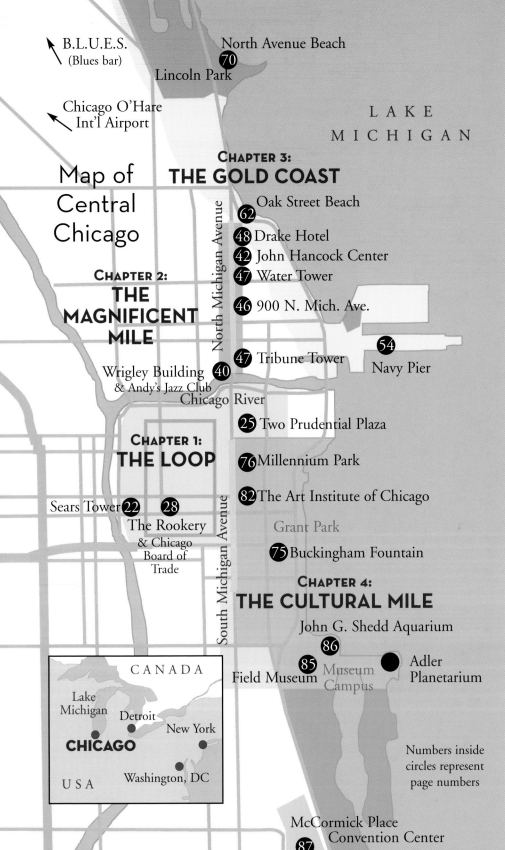

B.L.U.E.S.
(Blues bar)

North Avenue Beach

70 Lincoln Park

Chicago O'Hare
Int'l Airport

LAKE
MICHIGAN

Map of
Central
Chicago

CHAPTER 3:
THE GOLD COAST

Oak Street Beach

62

48 Drake Hotel

42 John Hancock Center

47 Water Tower

46 900 N. Mich. Ave.

North Michigan Avenue

CHAPTER 2:
THE MAGNIFICENT MILE

54

47 Tribune Tower

Navy Pier

40 Wrigley Building
& Andy's Jazz Club

Chicago River

25 Two Prudential Plaza

CHAPTER 1:
THE LOOP

76 Millennium Park

82 The Art Institute of Chicago

Sears Tower 22 28

The Rookery
& Chicago
Board of
Trade

Grant Park

South Michigan Avenue

75 Buckingham Fountain

CHAPTER 4:
THE CULTURAL MILE

John G. Shedd Aquarium

86

85 Museum Campus

Adler Planetarium

Field Museum

CANADA

Lake Michigan

Detroit

New York

CHICAGO

USA

Washington, DC

Numbers inside
circles represent
page numbers

McCormick Place
Convention Center

87

CHICAGO

Population of city (in 2006):	2,833,321
Year incoporated:	1837
Area of city:	237 square miles
Amount of lakefront shoreline:	31 miles
Altitude (feet above sea level):	586
Number of movable bridges:	46
Number of museums:	54
Number of parks:	550
Number of visitors (2006):	44 million

(Sources: U.S. Census, Chicago CTB, Wikipedia)

Renowned for restaurants and hospitality, Chicago offers a tantalizing array of food and beverage to visitor and resident alike. Here, servers at Wicker Park's Bongo Room and the Loop's Intelligentsia Café serve up mouth-watering specialities.

A Photo Tour of
CHICAGO

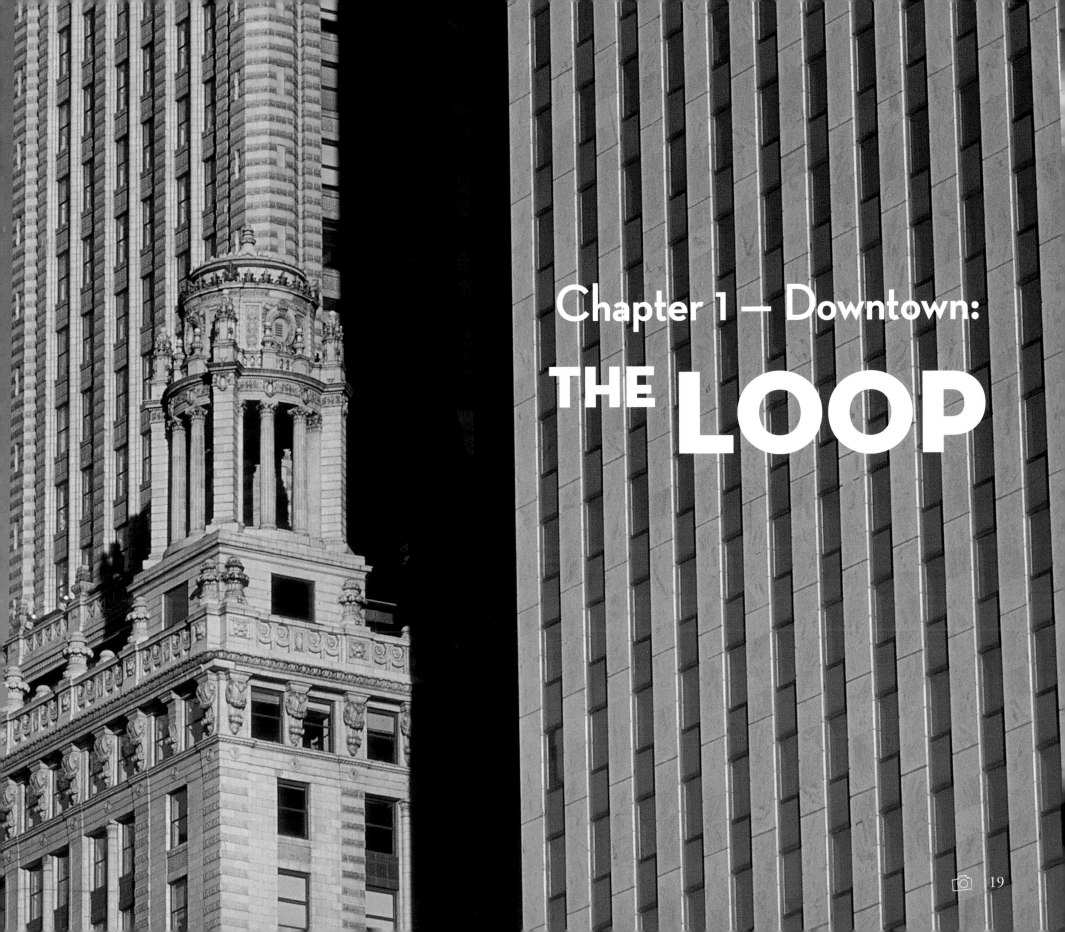

Chapter 1 — Downtown:
THE LOOP

THE LOOP

*"I have struck a city—a real city—
and they call it Chicago."*
—Rudyard Kipling,
'American Notes,' 1891.

In Chicago, all roads and train lines lead to the Loop, the historical center of the city. In 1897, four train companies connected together to form the Union Elevated Train Loop, encircling 35 city blocks of downtown and naming today's financial core "the Loop." Not even a square mile, the peninsula-like piece of land which the Loop occupies is bounded by Lake Michigan to the east and two branches of the Chicago River to the north and west.

Founded as Fort Dearborn, Chicago began life as a strategic trading site along the Great Lakes and Midwestern trading routes. In the 1880s and 90s, merchants Marshall Field, Aaron Montgomery Ward,

Richard Sears and Alvah Roebuck vied for the hearts and wallets of Midwesterners with general merchandise emporiums and mail-order catalogs. Today, the former headquarters of Sears, Roebuck and Co.— the 110-story Sears Tower—stands as the tallest building in the Western hemisphere.

The skyscraper is the dominant feature of Chicago's Loop, perhaps because it was born here. From the ashes of the Great Chicago Fire of 1871—which destroyed most downtown wooden buildings—rose William Le Baron Jenney's ten-story Home Insurance Building in 1885. With a blank slate to work with, and the twin developments of steel framing and electric elevators to exploit, Louis Sullivan, Daniel Burnham, and John Wellborn Root and other "Chicago School" architects of the 1890s made Chicago the birthplace of modern architecture. Today, a mass of skyscrapers thrusts upward from the flat Midwestern prairie and towers over the windswept waters of Lake Michigan.

Around it all rattles the "L"—an elevated train system developed since 1869 to literally rise above the problem of traffic congestion. Riding the "L" around the Loop provides a glimpse of Chicago's past, present and future.

Wacker Drive (along the Chicago River) and Michigan Avenue (to the left) form the northeastern edge of the Loop.

SEARS TOWER

"The Cheapest Supply House On Earth."
—*Title of the 'Sears, Roebuck & Co.' catalog of 1894.*

Icon of Chicago's skyline, the 110-story Sears Tower is North America's tallest building. Rising one quarter mile (1,450 feet / 442 meters) above the ground and sitting on two city blocks, Sears Tower comprises 4.5 million square feet of office and commercial space. The 103rd floor Skydeck is Chicago's highest observatory.

Sears Tower was the world's tallest building from its completion in 1973 to 1996. Today, that title is held by Taipei 101 in Taiwan (1,674 ft / 508 m, 101 stories, completed in 2004), although if its antenna could count (officially it can't), Sears Tower would still reign at 1,707 ft/ 527 m.

Richard Sears started selling watches in 1886, at age 22. With watch repairman Alvah Roebuck, he established Sears, Roebuck and Co. in Chicago in 1893, pioneering the mail-order catalog business with cross-town rival Aaron Montgomery Ward. Today, Sears Holdings is the world's largest department store and the country's third-largest retailer. Sears was headquartered in Sears Tower from 1973 to 1993, when it relocated 30 miles north-west to Hoffman Estates, Illinois.

Left: The dome of the Jewelers Building (1926) once held Al Capone's notorious speakeasy, the Stratosphere Club.

Above: Old Father Time atop the patina-washed 35 East Wacker Building clock has stood watch over Chicagoans since the building's completion in 1927.

Above: The Aon center (1973, center-right) is Chicago's second-tallest building. Nearby is Two Prudential Plaza (1990, triangular top). They both tower over the sailboats of Monroe Harbor.

Right: An "L" station straddles the city's State and Lake Streets in the Loop. The elevated tracks and stations in the Loop, built in 1895, are the oldest in the city.

Is it a woman or a dog? Pablo Picasso (1881–1973) didn't help by not titling his 1967 cubist work in Daley Plaza.

It's definitely a woman, although surreal and titled "Chicago" (1981). So said Spaniard Joan Miró (1893–1983) of his work at Brunswick Plaza.

"It was sort of pink and has a long neck" observed American sculptor Alexander Calder, calling his 53'-tall 1974 statue in the Federal Plaza "Flamingo."

staircase in the Rookery, which was named for the dirty pigeons and crooked politicians that inhabited the site's previous building, City Hall

Left: An icon of the 1930s, the Chicago Board of Trade continues to serve as a center for commodities trading, an industry pioneered in Chicago. Prominently featured in movies such as "The Untouchables," the 45-story Art Deco building opened in 1930 and served as the city's tallest structure for 40 years. It is crowned by a glimmering statue of Ceres, the Roman goddess of corn, grain and agriculture, and derivation of the word "cereal."

Above: The grand staircase of the Chicago Cultural Center (1893–97) is made of Carrara marble inset with medallions of rare emerald marble from Ireland. Once the city's main library, the Center is a showcase of concerts, plays and book readings.

Right: Made of mother-of-pearl and glittering colored glass, the world's largest Tiffany dome adorns the Chicago Cultural Center.

"She could see the smoke of the engines get lost
down where the streaks of steel flashed in the sun
and when the newspapers came in on the morning
mail she knew there was a big Chicago far off,
where all the trains ran."
—*From 'Mamie,' by Carl Sandburg, 1916.*

Riding the "L"—Chicago's elevated train. By the opening of the Civil War, more railroads met at Chicago than at any other spot on earth, making Chicago the transportation hub of America.

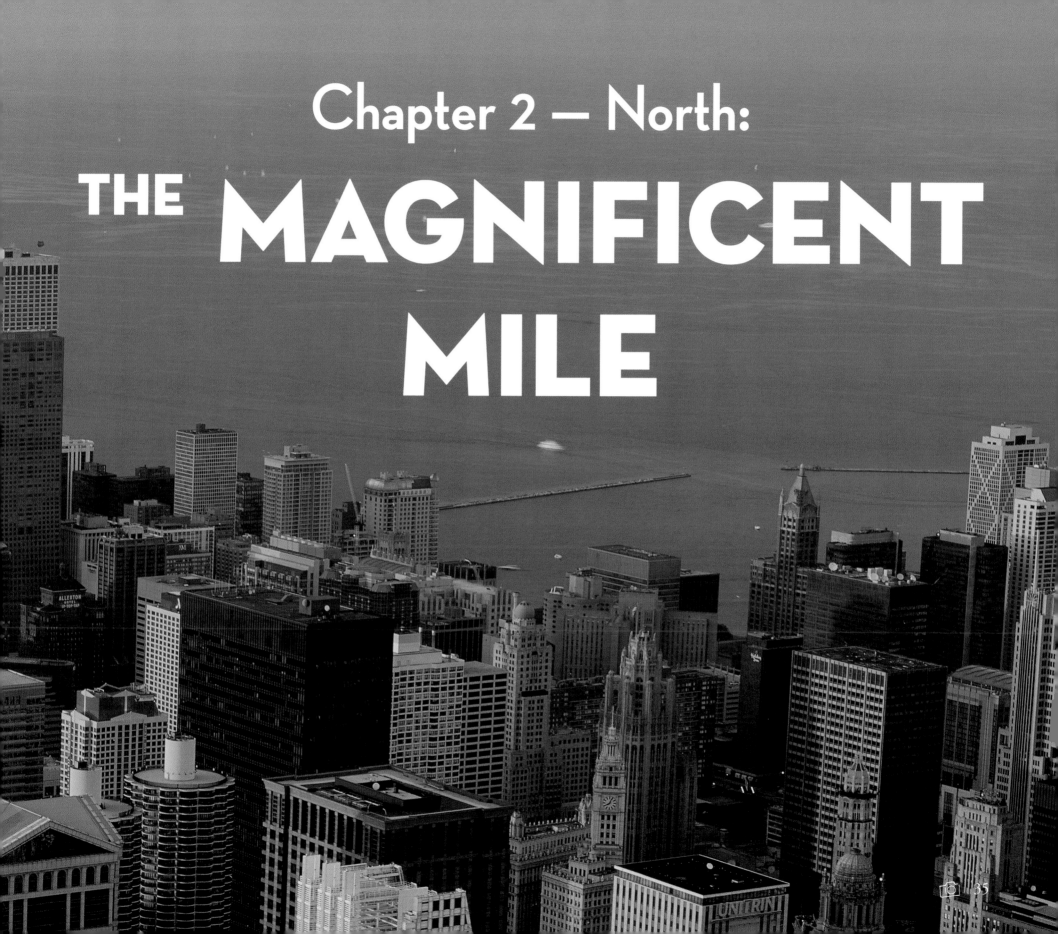

Chapter 2 — North:

THE MAGNIFICENT MILE

THE MAGNIFICENT MILE

"I'd rather be a lamppost in Chicago than a millionaire in any other city."
—William A. Hubert.

Shop **'til you drop** on Chicago's retail mecca—the Magnificent Mile. This is the marketing name of the one-mile-long stretch of North Michigan Avenue just north of the Loop from the Chicago River to Oak Street. Here, amongst tree-lined streets, the Mile boasts four shopping centers, 460 stores and 275 restaurants.

Exclusive retail establishments include Bloomingdale's, Neiman Marcus, Saks Fifth Avenue, Lord & Taylor, and Nordstrom. Prestigious boutiques include Cartier, Hermès, Giorgio Armani, and Tiffany & Co. And luxurious hotels include The Peninsula Chicago, Four Seasons Hotel Chicago, Park Hyatt, Le

Once a trading post, the area was re-imagined in the 1909 'Chicago Plan' as a major commercial boulevard, similar to the Champs Elysee in Paris. The streets were widened, a bridge was added, and the shoreline was stabilized with 125 acres of landfill to stop flooding.

At the start of the Magnificent Mile is where the original 1779 trading post which founded Chicago was located. The Roaring 1920s brought two landmark buildings here, both modeled after cathedrals—the 1924 Wrigley Building (after a Spanish cathedral), and the 1925 Chicago Tribune Building (modeled after a French gothic cathedral).

The name "The Magnificent Mile" comes from a 1947 promotion by Chicago developer Arthur Rubloff, who launched an extensive renovation and redevelopment plan to entirely revitalize the area.

One of the so-called Mag Mile's most recognizable landmarks is the 1870s Gothic Revival Water Tower (shown on page 45). The tower was one of the few structures to survive the Great Chicago Fire of 1871 and now serves as a captivating centerpiece and an icon for the neighborhood and city.

Across the Chicago River from the Loop, the Wrigley Building (right, white) commences The Magnificent Mile.

The First Lady and Little Lady take visitors on architectural cruises along the Chicago River.

WRIGLEY BUILDING

*"When two men in business always agree,
one of them is unnecessary."*
—*William Wrigley, Jr. (1861–1932).*

The gleaming white Wrigley Building — one of America's most famous office towers — stands on the banks of the Chicago River and serves as the southern anchor of the Magnificent Mile.

The 1924 building was modeled after the Giralda Tower of the cathedral in Seville, Spain and is capped with a massive four-faced clock. The surface is clad in 250,000 terra-cotta tiles, individually glazed with six shades of white enamel, ranging from cream at the base to blue-white at the top, so that the brightness of the building increases as it rises. The building consists of two towers, connected by a walkway on the 14th floor, and is the headquarters of chewing gum manufacturer, Wm. Wrigley Jr. Company.

At the age of 29, William Wrigley Jr. came to Chicago from Philadelphia in 1891 and gave away chewing gum as a

sales tool to sell baking powder. But the gum proved more popular and in 1893 he marketed Juicy Fruit and Wrigley's Spearmint gum. Today, the Wrigley Company is the world's largest manufacturer of chewing gum, with global sales of over $3 billion.

JOHN HANCOCK CENTER

"The British ministry can read that name
without spectacles."
—*John Hancock (1737-1793), about his large signature on*
the Declaration of Independence.

The boldest signature of Chicago's sky-line is appropriately named the John Hancock Center. Opened in 1969, the black obelisk is 100 stories tall.

On the 94th floor is the open-air "Skywalk" observatory, where you can breathe the air outside, hear the noise of the city over 1,000 feet below, and see up to 80 miles away and over four states.

The Hancock Center's distinctive X-bracing gives strength to an exterior shell, rather than an interior core, thereby increasing the usable space inside. The multi-use building contains a sky-view restaurant, America's highest swimming pool (on the 44th floor) and the world's highest residences (floors 44–92). The apartments are so high that when the residents are above the clouds they have to call the doorkeeper to ask what the weather is like at street-level.

The tower was built for, and named after, John Hancock Mutual Life Insurance Company of Boston (now a subsidiary of Canada's Manulife Financial Corporation). The company, formed in 1862, encouraged Americans to sign insurance contracts by taking the name of the first man to sign the Declaration of Independence in 1776.

GARI

Left and above: Like a palace in the sky, the tower of 900 North Michigan Avenue (1989) rises above the clouds. The structure is known as the "Bloomingdale's Building" for its anchor tenant. During the holidays, the seven-story atrium shopping mall is almost filled with a giant Christmas tree.

Two gothic landmarks. *Above:* Tribune Tower (1925)—home of the Chicago Tribune newspaper—is modeled after the Notre Dame cathedral in Rouen, France. The eight flying buttresses around the crown include sculptures of bats carved into them. The newspaper used a competition to find "the most beautiful and distinctive building in the world." Embedded in the walls are 120 rock fragments from famous sites such as the Alamo, Taj Mahal, Parthenon, Great Pyramid, Great Wall of China, Westminster Abbey, and even from the moon.

Right: The gothic Water Tower (1866–69) was one of five public buildings to survive the Great Chicago Fire of 1871 and became a symbol of the city's rebirth. Water from Lake Michigan was pumped up the 138-foot standpipe inside the tower to equalize water pressure around Chicago. Today, the tower is a visitors center.

Anchoring the northern end of the Magnificent Mile, the elegant Drake Hotel has been a symbol of white glove excellence since 1920.

The Gold Coast's Oak Street Beach is just steps from the Magnificent Mile.

Chapter 3 — North:
THE GOLD COAST

THE GOLD COAST

"Chicago, mistress of the lakes,
Controller of our inland trade,
The freest city of our states,
What wondrous strides thy fame has made!"
—Charles Frederick White, 'To Chicago.'

Neither the Oz-like towers of the Loop nor the prairie flatness of Chicago is as visually dominating, stunning or inspiring as the broad, blue vastness of Lake Michigan. The only one of the five Great Lakes contained wholly within the United States, Lake Michigan serves as dramatic, churning backdrop to the city in winter months; and soothing, placid doorstep in the summer.

In 1779, the city's first European settler, Jean Baptiste Du Sable, established a fur-trading post at the mouth of today's Chicago River, which connected the water routes of the mid-continent to the open-waters of the Great Lakes. For early Chicagoans, Lake Michigan was a source of trade and prosperity, as well as perch, salmon and fresh water.

When sewage dumped in the Chicago River started polluting the drinking water of Lake Michigan—killing 12 percent of the city's population with cholera and typhoid in 1885—civic planners employed a bold, expensive and quintessentially Chicago remedy—reversing the flow of the river. In 1900, a 28-mile-long canal opened to the Des Plaines River, taking sewage south instead of north, all the way to the Gulf of Mexico.

Today, the Chicago River slices through the city center and serves as nautical highway for pleasure mariners heading out to the lake on summer weekends. Jammed with ice on winter days, and dyed green on St. Patrick's Day, the river flows with canoeists, kayakers, crew teams, and even Venetian gondoliers.

The Gold Coast (and the adjoining neighborhood of Streeterville) is the lakefront area north of the river, replete with golden beaches. For the city's nearly three million residents, the Lake and the Gold Coast provide legroom, oxygen and play-space.

NAVY PIER

"When asked what I am most proud of, I stick out my chest, hold my head high and state proudly, 'I served in the United States Navy!'"
—*John F. Kennedy, 35th US president (1917–63).*

Over 8 million visitors a year make Navy Pier Chicago's most popular year-round attraction. Opened as the world's largest pier in 1916, Navy Pier juts 3,000 feet over Lake Michigan and is named to honor World War I veterans. Once the home to Lake Michigan freighters, the pier was renovated in 1994 to become a 50-acre playground.

The list of attractions is almost as long as the pier itself. At the entrance is the 19-acre Gateway Park with a 240-jet computerized granite fountain, and a Children's Museum in the Headhouse building (1916). Further along is an 18-hole Chicago-themed miniature golf course; a funhouse maze; an IMAX theater with a 6-story-high screen; the Smith Museum featuring 150 stained-glass windows; and the one-acre Crystal Gardens with over 70 full-size palm trees. At the far end, the Auditorium (1916) houses the Grand Ballroom with a 100-foot-high half-domed ceiling.

The centerpiece is a 148-foot-high Ferris wheel which, at night, is illuminated with thousands of sparkling lights.

The 148-foot-high Ferris wheel was modeled after the world's first such wheel which made its debut at Chicago's 1893 World's Columbian Exposition.

Riders are flung through the air on the colorful Wave Swinger. Adjacent is Crystal Gardens, a one-acre indoor palm court enclosed in a glass atrium.

The speedy "Seadog" embarks, or perhaps em-barks, from Navy Pier.

The Chicago Harbor Lighthouse, built in 1893, guards the outer breakwater of the Chicago River.

The Beaches of Chicago.

Above and immediate right: Just steps from the Magnificent Mile and the John Hancock Center lies Oak Street Beach. Chicago's most famous beach may be man-made with imported sand but it's a great place to watch runners, bikers and bladers.

Far left, right, and following page: North Avenue Beach is a vast expanse of sun, sand and sunbathing along Lake Shore Drive. Sand volleyball courts, extensive beaches, a chess pavilion, an in-line skating rink, and running and bike trails, make this beach the favorite of North Siders. The whole show can be overseen by revelers on the upper deck of the North Avenue Beach House (2000), a two-story building designed to look like an ocean liner.

Howard Scott and the World Band play at the intimate B.L.U.E.S., voted best blues club on Chicago's North Side since 1979.

Local artist Son Seals (since passed away) plays the packed room at B.L.U.E.S., which features cold beer and hot blues in close quarters.

Andy's Jazz Club on Hubbard Street in River North is a downtown jazz standard for the after-work crowd.

An 1886 monument to German poet Friedrich Schiller overlooks the Conservatory (1895).

LINCOLN PARK

"The people's resort."
—*Illinois Legislature, in creating Lincoln Park, 1869.*

"Whatever you are, be a good one."
—*Abraham Lincoln (1809–65).*

In a city of parks, the largest is Lincoln Park, at 1,208 acres. Originally a public cemetery for victims of cholera and smallpox, the land was converted to a park in 1860 and named, shortly thereafter, for president Abraham Lincoln (1809–65). Expansions and landfills through the 1950s brought the area to its present size.

Sitting in the heart of Lincoln Park, within sight and striking distance of Lake Michigan's cooling breezes, is Lincoln Park Zoo. Established in 1868 with a gift of two swans, Lincoln Park Zoo is the nation's oldest free public zoo, and the only remaining free cultural institution in Chicago. Drawing over three million visitors a year, the Zoo is Chicago's second-most visited attraction, after Navy Pier, and is known for its gorillas and primates.

Just north of the Zoo is the Victorian-style Conservatory, completed in 1895, which houses over 20,000 orchids as well as palms, ferns and other exotic tropicals.

The park contains 15 baseball areas, 6 basketball courts, 2 softball courts, 35 tennis courts, 163 volley-ball courts, land-scaped gardens, a theater on the lake, and a butterfly house.

Paddle boats ply the waters of South Pond in Lincoln Park.

Chapter 4 — South:

THE CULTURAL MILE

THE CULTURAL MILE

The "intellectual center of Chicago."
—Daniel Burnham, about Grant Park, 1909.

Most of the major museums of Chicago reside around "the Cultural Mile." A name adopted by the City of Chicago in 2004, the Cultural Mile is a counterpoint to the commercial Magnificent Mile to the north, and includes a one-mile stretch of South Michigan Avenue and Grant Park.

Known as Chicago's "front yard," Grant Park features grand promenades and geometric designs modeled after the gardens of Versailles in France. Established in 1836, the park was expanded by landfill when debris from the 1871 fire was dumped into Lake Michigan. Renamed in 1901 for the 18th U.S. president, Ulysses S. Grant, the park was saved from develop-ment by Chicago mail-order magnate Aaron Montgomery Ward who fought a 20-year legal battle until 1911 to keep the park "forever open, clear and free." Landfill has since extended Grant Park east with Museum Campus and north-west with Millennium Park.

The greenery of Grant Park extends south to Jackson Park, home of the Museum of Science and Industry and the main site for the 1893 World's Columbian Exposition.

More than any other event, the 1893 World's Columbian Exposition transformed Chicago. Creating a "White City" of neo-classical exposition buildings, set amidst lagoons and parklands designed by Frederick Law Olmsted, exposition plan-ners led by Chicagoan Daniel Hudson Burnham spawned a City Beautiful move-ment that improved the architecture of Chicago and other cities across America.

Using materials collected and built for the Exposition, Chicago's leading citi-zens began creating some of the world's largest museums. Today's citizens and visi-tors now enjoy the Field Museum of Natural History, the John G. Shedd Aquarium, and the Adler Planetarium on the Museum Campus of Grant Park.

Another Chicago icon, the Clarence Buckingham Fountain (1927) contains three pink marble basins, four bronze sea horses, 133 jets of water, hundreds of spotlights, and 1.5 million gallons of water. The fountain is the centerpiece of Grant Park which was modeled after the gardens of Versailles.

MILLENNIUM PARK

"Chicago, the wonder city, has a new wonder."
—*Chicago Tribune, 18 July, 2004.*

Opened with great fanfare and acclaim in 2004, Millennium Park serves as the verdant and cutting-edge centerpiece to Chicago's Cultural Mile. Combining sculptures, gardens, and a performance center, Millennium Park draws people to interactive modern art that invoke all five senses. Get wet in the Crown Fountain, listen to music in the outdoor theater, eat at the Park Grill, smell the perennials at Lurie Garden, and see the sky and yourself in "the Bean."

Once an ugly railyard, this $475M project is now a 24-acre northern expansion of Grant Park. Collaborators read like a contemporary Who's Who of design, including American architect Frank Gehry with his Pritzker Pavilion and ribbon-like bridge, Anish Kapoor and his 110-ton, reflective Cloud Gate sculpture (also known as "the Bean"), and Jaume Plensa and his double-tower multimedia Crown Fountain.

The faces of more than 1,000 Chicagoans appear on the Crown Fountain.

Children love getting wet in the Crown Fountain (2004)—a pair of 50'-high glass towers of water and video, connected by a 232'-long reflecting pool. Each face is displayed for 12 minutes, and ends its reign by pursing its lips and "spitting" like a gargoyle on excited children.

Officially called "Cloud Gate" (2004), this stainless steel sculpture by Indian-born and London-based Anish Kapoor is affectionately known as "the Bean."

Relaxing in the park of art. The billowing steel panels of Frank Gehry's Jay Pritzker Pavilion appear as though the music has burst through a wall.

A night-time orchestral performance in the outdoor Jay Pritzker Pavilion (2004), an acoustical and architectural wonder.

THE ART INSTITUTE OF CHICAGO

"Art is long, life is short."
(Ars Longa, Vita Brevis)
—Hippocrates, Greek writer (circa 460–377 BC).

The entrance on South Michigan Avenue is guarded by bronze lions (1892).

Some of the world's most famous artworks entrance the visitor at The Art Institute of Chicago. Art-lovers can view Grant Wood's *American Gothic* (1930), Edward Hopper's *Nighthawks* (1942), Seurat's *Sunday Afternoon on the Island of La Grande Jatte*, as well as works by Monet, Pablo Picasso, Henri Matisse, Salvador Dalí, Jackson Pollock, and Andy Warhol. The Art Institute contains the city's largest, oldest and most comprehensive collection of art, including the second-largest collection of Impressionist paintings after Paris' Louvre.

The Art Institute of Chicago, founded in 1879 as both a museum and school, opened in its present Beaux-Arts main building on Michigan Avenue and Adams Street in 1893. The collection now encompasses more than 5,000 years of human expression from cultures around the world, and the school's graduate program is continually ranked as one of the best in the country.

Admiring "Paris Street; Rainy Day, 1877" by Gustave Caillebotte at The Art Institute of Chicago.

The grandeur of ancient Rome welcomes visitors to the Field Museum, housed in Daniel Burnham's 1921 neo-classical temple of white marble.

THE FIELD MUSEUM

*"The distance is nothing;
it's only the first step that is difficult."*
—Marshall Field (1834–1906), museum benefactor.

The Field Museum of Natural History is one of the world's great museums, with over 20 million anthropological, botanical, geological and zoological specimens. Yet, with all this to offer, many people visit for one exhibit—Sue, the largest, most complete, and best preserved Tyrannosaurus Rex fossil yet discovered.

Sue was named for fossil hunter Sue Hendrickson, who discovered the bones in 1990 in a sandstone cliff in South Dakota. The Field Museum (with the help of McDonald's and Walt Disney World) acquired Sue in 1997 at a Sotheby's auction for $7.6 million. Most of the money went to the landowner where the skeleton was found—none went to the original Sue or her fellow discovers.

The Field Museum was founded in 1893 as the Columbian Museum of Chicago, to house the biological and anthropological collections of the World's Columbian Exposition. The name was changed in 1905 to honor a major benefactor, department store magnate Marshall Field.

Born in Massachusetts, Marshall Field (1834–1906) moved to Chicago in 1856 and founded Marshall Field and Co. (1881), one of the world's largest department stores. Amassing one of the largest private fortunes in the United States, Field gave nine million dollars to the Field Museum, and also founded the University of Chicago.

Sue, a 67-million-year-old T. Rex skeleton, is over 90% complete.

At O'Hare International Airport, passengers travel through art between the B and C concourses of Terminal One. The world's second-busiest airport (after Atlanta), O'Hare is named for World War II naval pilot hero and Chicagoan, Edward "Butch" O'Hare.

Boarding a Red Line train on Chicago's subway.

Pedestrian reflections on Diversey Parkway in the Lincoln Park neighborhood.

Forging the steel that made Chicago, at A. Finkl & Sons.

Solitude and standing. Viewing Lake Michigan from Milton Lee Olive Park.

Thanks for taking a photo tour of Chicago.